ASTRONOMY LAB

Explore Space with Art & Activities

STEAM LAB

Elsie Olson

Checkerboard Library

An Imprint of Abdo Publishing
abdobooks.com

abdobooks.com

Printed in the United States of America, North Mankato, Minnesota
052023
092023

THIS BOOK CONTAINS
RECYCLED MATERIALS

Design: Tamara JM Peterson, Mighty Media, Inc.
Editor: Megan Borgert-Spaniol
Cover Photographs: Mighty Media, Inc. (project photos); Pixel-Shot/Shutterstock (child)
Interior Photographs: Andrey Boyarskiy/Shutterstock, pp. 6 (sieve), 7 (sieve); AstroStar/Shutterstock, p. 5; Denis Belitsky/ Shutterstock, p. 17; Jiang Zhongyan/Shutterstock, p. 6 (cardboard tubes); Jiri Hera/Shutterstock, p. 6 (flour); Mighty Media, Inc., pp. 6, 7, 10, 11, 14, 18, 19, 22, 26, 27; milart/Shutterstock, p. 6 (tights); NASA, pp. 9, 13, 25; NASA/ESA/ Flickr, p. 21; NASA/Flickr, p. 29; Oleksii Grygorenko/Shutterstock, p. 6 (buttons); PHLD Luca/Shutterstock, p. 6 (electrical tape); Spalnic/Shutterstock, p. 6 (paint); Voravuth Chuanyou/Shutterstock, pp. 6 (stir sticks), 7 (stir sticks).
Design Elements: korzuen/Shutterstock; Olga Zuevskaya/Shutterstock; pro500/Shutterstock; projectdezyn/Shutterstock

Library of Congress Control Number: 2022949250

Publisher's Cataloging-in-Publication Data

Names: Olson, Elsie, author.
Title: Astronomy lab: explore space with art & activities / by Elsie Olson
Other title: explore space with art & activities
Description: Minneapolis, Minnesota : Abdo Publishing, 2024 | Series: STEAM lab | Includes online resources and index.
Identifiers: ISBN 9781098291587 (lib. bdg.) | ISBN 9781098278045 (ebook)
Subjects: LCSH: Science--Juvenile literature. | Handicraft--Juvenile literature. | Science projects--Juvenile literature. | Astronomy--Juvenile literature. | Space--Juvenile literature.
Classification: DDC 507.8--dc23

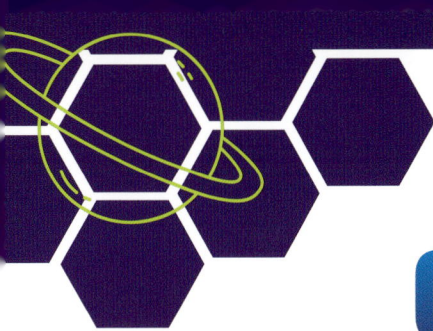

CONTENTS

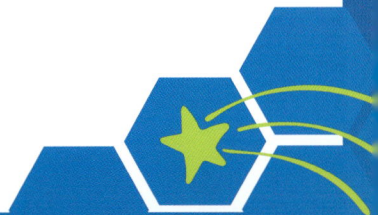

ASTRONOMY LAB

Have you ever found yourself staring up at the night sky and imagining what might be out there? Maybe you imagine yourself exploring faraway **exoplanets** and searching for alien life. If so, you may be a budding astronomer!

Astronomers are scientists who study outer space. This includes **celestial** bodies, such as stars, moons, and planets. Astronomers also study distant **galaxies** and mysterious **black holes**. They work to unravel some of science's greatest mysteries, such as how the universe began!

The projects in this book will introduce you to astronomy using art and activities. You'll **simulate** crater formation on our moon, make black hole art, and more! So, turn on your curiosity and point your telescope to the sky. The astronomy lab is open for discovery!

Scientists estimate there are one septillion stars in the observable universe. That number is written with a one followed by 24 zeros!

LAB PREP

Astronomers rely on telescopes, space **probes**, and powerful computers to study stars and planets. To do the projects in this book, you will need a few tools too!

- ✔ buttons
- ✔ cardboard tubes
- ✔ coffee stir sticks
- ✔ electrical tape
- ✔ flashlight
- ✔ flour
- ✔ food dye
- ✔ marbles
- ✔ paint
- ✔ sequins
- ✔ sifter or sieve
- ✔ tights or nylons

Lab Rules

All research labs have a set of rules its scientists must follow. Here are some rules to help you stay safe and have fun in your own astronomy lab!

- ✔ Ask permission before you start, and ask for help when you get stuck.
- ✔ Read the instructions and gather all your supplies before starting a project.
- ✔ Stay safe when using sharp or hot materials.
- ✔ Clean up when you are done and put everything away.
- ✔ Be creative with these projects. Find ways to make them your own!

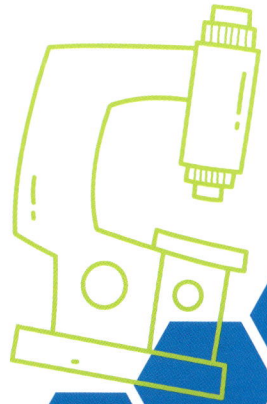

MEET YOUR MOON

Have you ever gazed up at the sky on a clear night?
If so, there's a good chance you saw the speckled, glowing face of the moon shining back at you. The moon is planet Earth's closest **celestial** neighbor. It is the brightest object in our night sky. It is also the only surface besides Earth that humans have traveled to!

Scientists think the moon formed when a Mars-sized planet crashed into Earth. The debris eventually came together into a natural **satellite**. This happened billions of years ago. And the moon has been helping us ever since! The moon's **gravitational** pull helps keep Earth from wobbling too much as it rotates. This keeps our climate stable, giving Earth regular seasons. The moon's gravity also pulls on our planet's oceans, causing tides.

Astronauts last set foot on the moon in 1972. The moonwalkers' footprints are still intact!

MAKE A CRATER

The surface of the moon is covered with bowl-shaped holes called craters. These were formed when comets, asteroids, and meteors crashed into the moon. Use everyday kitchen ingredients to create your own mini **impact** event!

What You Need

- ✔ baking dish
- ✔ flour
- ✔ ruler
- ✔ sequins
- ✔ measuring cup
- ✔ mixing bowl
- ✔ food dye
- ✔ plastic gloves
- ✔ sifter
- ✔ newspaper or plastic sheet
- ✔ small rocks

What You Do

1 Fill the baking dish with flour so the flour is between 1 and 2 inches (2.5 and 5 cm) deep. This layer represents the lower mantle of the moon's surface.

2 Sprinkle sequins on top of the flour. This layer represents the upper mantle of the moon's surface.

3 Pour about 1 cup flour into the mixing bowl and add several drops of food dye. Use gloved hands to rub the food dye into the flour. Add more dye if needed.

4 Sift the colored flour into the baking dish to cover the sequins. This colored layer represents the crust of the moon's surface.

5 You're ready to drop craters on the moon! Set the baking dish on the floor or ground. Remember to use newspaper or a plastic sheet to protect your surface.

6 Hold the rocks high above the dish and drop them onto your moon surface one at a time. Observe how all three layers of the moon's surface are disrupted. The **impact** of each rock creates a crater!

LAB FACT
The moon has no atmosphere and no weather. This means there is no erosion to erase the craters. Any impact scar is there to stay!

SUPER SOLAR SYSTEM

The solar system is our cosmic neighborhood. It includes all the planets, asteroids, comets, and other objects that orbit our home star, the sun. Many planets have their own moons. Some have more than 50 moons each!

Earth is one of eight planets in the solar system. Venus is the closest planet to Earth. But it's still as far as 162 million miles (261 million km) away! In 1970, it took a Soviet Union spacecraft more than three months to get there. The farthest planet from Earth is Neptune. It took a **NASA** spacecraft from 2006 to 2014 to reach Neptune's orbit!

If you started flying to Neptune today, how old would you be when you arrived there?

More than 1,300 Earths would fit inside the largest planet, Jupiter.

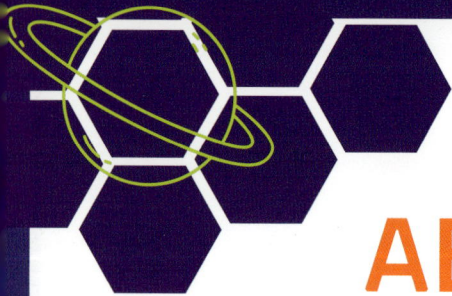

ABSTRACT PLANET ART

Mercury, Venus, Earth, and Mars are the closest planets to the sun. They have solid, rocky surfaces. Farther away are Jupiter, Saturn, Uranus, and Neptune. These planets are made almost entirely of gas and have no surfaces. Make an artistic model of the planets using buttons and wooden sticks!

What You Need

- ✔ internet or books for research
- ✔ 8 buttons of varying size
- ✔ paint & paintbrushes
- ✔ glitter
- ✔ wire
- ✔ wire cutter
- ✔ hot glue
- ✔ jar lid
- ✔ coffee stir sticks
- ✔ scissors
- ✔ magnet (optional)

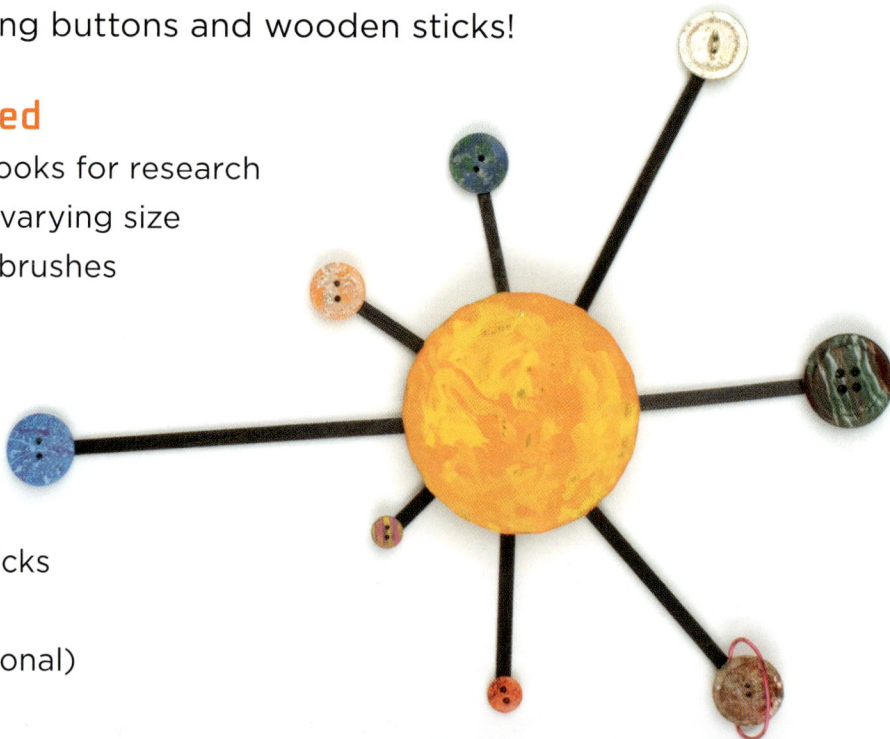

What You Do

1 Research the size of the eight planets in the solar system. Choose a button to represent each planet based on its size.

2 Paint the planets! Make swirls, stripes, dots, and splatters. Add glitter to some planets. Let the paint dry.

3 Cut a small length of wire and wrap it around Saturn to make a ring. Glue the wire ends to the back of the button.

4 Paint the jar lid to look like the sun and let it dry.

5 For each planet, cut a stir stick according to its distance from the sun. For example, Neptune's stick should be the longest, as it is farthest from the sun. Mercury's stick should be the shortest, as it is closest to the sun.

6 Glue one end of each stick to the back of its planet. Glue the other end of the stick to the back of the sun.

7 Display your solar system! If you'd like, glue a magnet to the back of the sun so your artwork can hang on a refrigerator or inside a locker.

LAB FACT
Dwarf planet Pluto orbits the sun just beyond Neptune. Pluto was considered a ninth planet until 2006, when astronomers **reclassified** it. Some astronomers believe there may be a Neptune-sized planet lurking far beyond Pluto!

THE SUN & OTHER STARS

A star is a hot ball of gas that gives off light and heat. The night sky is full of visible stars. But you can also see one big star during the day. It's the sun!

The sun is the star of our solar system. It provides the light and warmth that make life on Earth possible. Without the sun, we wouldn't be here. Nor would the entire solar system!

The sun is a medium-sized star. It is 12 times bigger than a red dwarf, the smallest star type. But the largest type of star, a red supergiant, can be up to 1,000 times larger than the sun! The sun may be special to us. But compared to other stars, it's pretty average!

Locate the brightest star in the night sky and track its movement. Does its location change over the course of a week? A month? A year?

There are at least 100 billion stars in our home galaxy, the Milky Way.

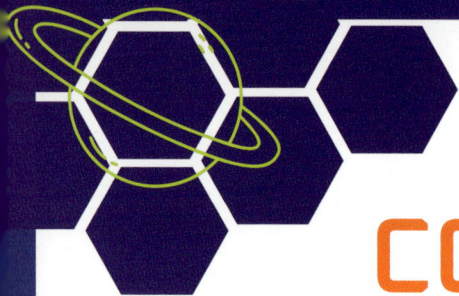

CONSTELLATION PROJECTOR

An estimated 6,000 stars can be seen from Earth without a telescope. For thousands of years, humans have found patterns in these stars. These patterns are called constellations. Create a projector to display your favorite constellations!

What You Need

- ✔ flashlight
- ✔ pencil
- ✔ paperboard
- ✔ scissors
- ✔ dark paint & paintbrush (optional)
- ✔ internet or books for research
- ✔ black marker
- ✔ craft knife
- ✔ ruler
- ✔ electrical tape
- ✔ rubber band

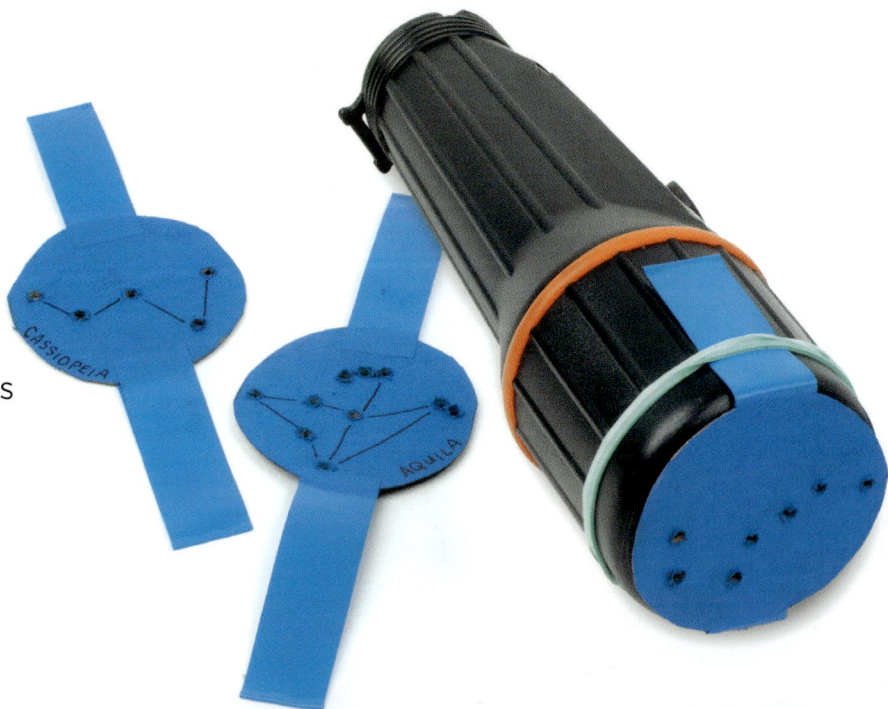

What You Do

1 Trace the lens of the flashlight on the paperboard and cut out the circle. Repeat this step for each constellation you want to create.

2 If your paperboard is a light color, paint both sides of the paperboard circles a dark color. Let the paint dry.

3 Look at reference images of constellations. Draw dots to represent a constellation's stars on one side of each circle. Use the craft knife to turn each dot into a hole.

4 Write the constellation name on each circle. Connect the holes with lines to show the constellation shape.

5 Cut two 6-inch (15 cm) strips of electrical tape for each circle. Attach one end of a strip to the paperboard. Fold the tape in half, attaching the other end to the flip side of the paperboard. This makes a flap. Repeat with the second strip of tape on the opposite side of the circle.

6 Set a paperboard circle over the flashlight's lens. Fold the tape flaps down and use a rubber band to hold them in place.

7 Turn out the lights and turn on the flashlight! Aim the light at a wall. Do you see your constellation?

LAB FACT
Humans have used stars and constellations to track the seasons and navigate the ocean.

19

OUR AMAZING UNIVERSE

The universe is a gigantic and mysterious place. It is home to billions of **galaxies**, trillions of stars, and even more planets. It contains everything that exists.

Scientists believe the universe was formed 12 to 14 billion years ago during an event called the big bang. At the start of the big bang, the entire universe was contained in a single very hot and very **dense** point. This point expanded to create a universe that is still expanding today. Astronomers and **astrophysicists** work hard to understand the universe and its secrets. But they still have many unanswered questions!

What is a question you have about the universe? How can you try to find an answer to your question?

The powerful Hubble Space Telescope allows scientists to view galaxies that formed just 600 million years after the big bang.

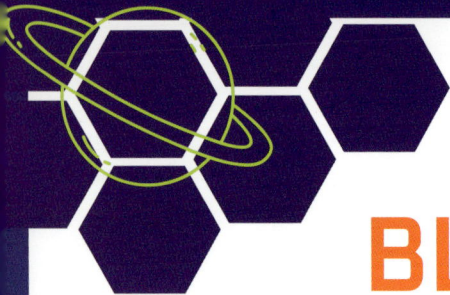

BLACK HOLE ART

Black holes are one of the universe's greatest mysteries. Scientists believe they are formed when stars much bigger than our sun collapse on themselves. This collapse creates a **gravitational** pull strong enough to swallow anything that comes too close, including light! Use a simple model of a black hole to create some beautifully messy black hole art.

What You Need

- ✔ tights or nylons
- ✔ scissors
- ✔ marbles
- ✔ twist tie or thin wire
- ✔ cylindrical container, pitcher, or bucket
- ✔ paint in various colors

What You Do

1 Cut one leg off the tights. Fill the toe with 10 to 15 marbles.

2 Pull the material tight around the marbles and secure it with the twist tie.

3 Set the marbles in the container. Pull the material around the container's rim and then all the way down the outside of the container. Keep pulling until the material stretches very tightly across the top. The weight of the marbles should pull the center of the material down. This represents the gravity of a **black hole**.

4 Practice rolling a marble just inside the rim of the container. The marble will roll in toward the center. This represents the way a black hole's gravity pulls objects in space toward it.

5 Dip a marble into one paint color and roll it onto the material. Watch it make swirls of color in toward the black hole.

6 Repeat step 5 with other marbles and paint colors as many times as you'd like.

LAB FACT
In 1916, **physicist** Albert Einstein first **predicted** the existence of black holes. It wasn't until 2019 that astronomers released the first photo of a black hole!

SEEING INTO SPACE

The universe is enormous. It would take our fastest spacecraft 18,000 years to reach the nearest star beyond the sun. If the spacecraft could travel at the speed of light, it would still take more than four years to reach the star.

Visiting faraway star systems isn't possible with current **technology**. So, scientists rely on other methods to learn about the universe. Astronomers send **probes** to fly past the planets in our solar system. Researchers have even sent robots called rovers to explore the surface of Mars. Astronomers use telescopes to peer at stars and **galaxies** far beyond our solar system. They also use math and **physics** calculations to understand parts of the universe that can't be seen.

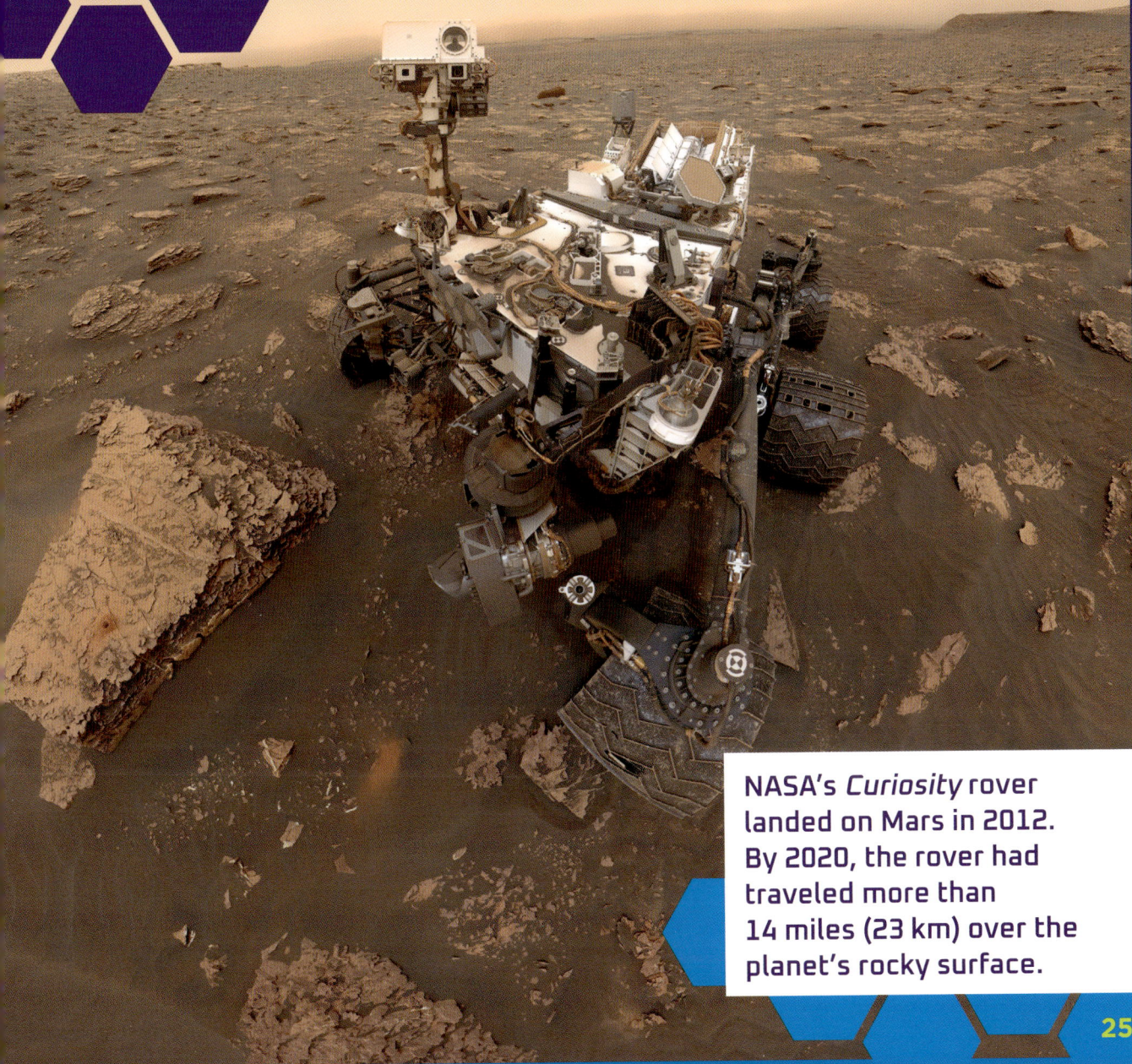

NASA's *Curiosity* rover landed on Mars in 2012. By 2020, the rover had traveled more than 14 miles (23 km) over the planet's rocky surface.

TELESCOPE SIMULATOR

Telescopes are among the most important tools for exploring the universe. They allow viewers to zoom in and out on **celestial** objects. Become an astronomer by building your own telescope that **simulates** this function!

What You Need

- ✔ 2 paper towel tubes
- ✔ scissors
- ✔ masking tape
- ✔ paint & paintbrushes
- ✔ clear plastic container, bottle, or sheet
- ✔ glitter glue
- ✔ craft foam
- ✔ hot glue
- ✔ 3 wooden chopsticks or dowels
- ✔ chenille stems

What You Do

1 Cut one paper towel tube down its length. Roll the tube slightly and tuck it halfway into the other paper towel tube. Release the inner tube so it expands and tape its seam together at the end. Remove the inner tube and tape along its entire seam. Paint both paper towel tubes and let them dry.

2 Trace one end of the narrower tube on the clear plastic. Cut out the circle. Use glitter glue to paint a **cosmic** scene on the circle. Let it dry.

3 Cut three strips of craft foam. Glue one around each end of the wider tube.

4 Glue the third strip around one end of the narrow tube. Glue your cosmic scene to the narrow tube's other end.

5 Insert the narrow tube end that holds the cosmic image into the wider tube. The combined tubes are your telescope!

6 Paint the chopsticks and let them dry. Use chenille stems to bind them together at one end into a tripod. Use more chenille stems to secure the telescope's wider end to the tripod.

7 Look through the wide tube. Pull and push the narrow tube to **simulate** zooming in and out!

ASTRONOMERS AT WORK

Astronomers can have many different jobs. They may become professors and share their knowledge with students. They may do research to answer big questions, such as which **exoplanets** could support life or what is inside a **black hole**. Some astronomers have even become astronauts who explore space in person!

No matter where their careers take them, all astronomers use creativity, problem-solving, and teamwork. These are the same skills you practice in school, at home, and by doing the projects in this book. Maybe one day, you will use these skills to explore space as an astronomer!

NASA astronaut Megan McArthur reads while orbiting above the northern Atlantic Ocean in the International Space Station.

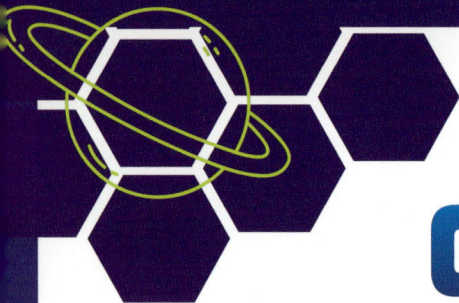

GLOSSARY

astrophysicist—a scientist who studies astrophysics, the study of the behavior and measurements of objects outside Earth's atmosphere.

black hole—an area of space where the gravity is so strong that light cannot escape.

celestial—positioned in or relating to the sky, or outer space as observed in astronomy.

cosmic—of or having to do with the universe apart from Earth.

dense—closely packed together or crowded.

exoplanet—a planet that exists outside of our solar system.

galaxy—a very large group of stars, planets, and other objects in space. The Earth is in a galaxy called the Milky Way.

gravitational—relating to movement toward a center of gravity.

impact—the forceful striking of one thing against another.

light-year—the distance that light travels in one year.

NASA—the National Aeronautics and Space Administration. NASA is a US government agency that manages the nation's space program and conducts flight research.

physicist—a person who studies physics. Physics is the science of how energy and objects affect each other.

predict—to guess something ahead of time based on observation, experience, or reasoning.

probe—a device used to explore and send back information.

reclassify—to assign to a different class or category.

satellite—an object, either natural or manufactured, that orbits a celestial body.

simulate—to imitate.

technology—machinery and equipment developed for practical purposes using scientific principles and engineering.

ONLINE RESOURCES

Booklinks
NONFICTION NETWORK
FREE! ONLINE NONFICTION RESOURCES

To learn more about astronomy, please visit **abdobooklinks.com** or scan this QR code. These links are routinely monitored and updated to provide the most current information available.

INDEX